One Who Stayed

One Who Stayed

Religious Life

Sister Mary J. Steinkamp, SNJM

Sister Mary J. Steinkamp

Essence
PUBLISHING

Belleville, Ontario, Canada

ONE WHO STAYED
Copyright © 2004, Sister Mary J. Steinkamp, SNJM

Library and Archives Canada Cataloguing in Publication

Steinkamp, Mary J. (Mary Julia), 1931-
     One who stayed : religious life / Mary J. Steinkamp.
ISBN 1-55306-783-5

     1. Steinkamp, Mary J. (Mary Julia), 1931- 2. Nuns-- United
States--Biography. I. Title.

BX4705.S86A3 2004   271'.9002   C2004-902992-4

To order more copies of this book, please contact:
Sister Mary J. Steinkamp SNJM
2014 NE 19th Avenue
Portland, OR 97212 USA

Essence Publishing is a Christian Book Publisher dedicated to furthering the work of Christ through the written word. For more information, contact:

20 Hanna Court, Belleville, Ontario, Canada K8P 5J2.
Phone: 1-800-238-6376. Fax: (613) 962-3055.
E-mail: publishing@essencegroup.com
Internet: www.essencegroup.com

Printed in Canada
by

Essence
PUBLISHING

DEDICATION

I dedicated this book to:

Blessed Marie Rose Durocher, who taught us that Jesus and Mary are our strength and our glory.

Sister Mary Breiling, whose faith, community spirit, and consideration inspire me.

Sister Barbara Bray, whose playful humor, bounce, and friendship are precious to me.

Patty and Cindy, whose generosity is beautiful.

Sister Anne Toback, who has the courage of her convictions.

Julie S. and Sandy T., whose love and respect for the children they teach make school a happy place.

Pamela Stone, whose goodness and kindness help me.

Sister Diane Hollcraft, whose prayers and healing touch enable me to write.

Sister Mary Lou DiJulio, who never ceases to dance into one's heart.

Sister Jeanne Concannon, whose unique wit, friendship, and poetic gifts have been a blessing to me.

TABLE OF CONTENTS

PREFACE

We are living in a world where people tend to make nuns into saints or demons. My book is an attempt to help people   realize that nuns are human, living in the real world, facing the shortcomings and goodness of the human race, in need of forgiveness like anyone else, and capable of tremendous good.

I wrote this book as a protest against the *I Leapt Over the Wall* books about religious life. I can't think of anything more beautiful than to dedicate one's life to God in religious life, in the married or single state. It is possible in all three vocations.

I think it is important to be realistic about human failings but to always look for what is good, true, and beautiful. As the song "Blessed Assurance" says, we need to be "filled with His goodness, lost in His love."

BEGINNINGS

The year was 1945. The place was a small town called Gervais about twenty miles from Salem, in a three-room school called Sacred Heart. I was young, merely an eighth-grader, talking to my teacher, Sister Raphael, about being a nun. She was very encouraging and did her best to direct me to the boarding school in Beaverton run by her SSMO order. I felt pushed; I balked. In my heart, I felt certain that I wanted to become a nun, but knowing which order or work to choose seemed as remote as the stars and as distant as the planets. I pulled back at her suggestion and followed my brothers to Sacred Heart Academy in Salem, run by a different order—Holy Names Sisters. I was very careful not to talk to any of these Sisters about my plans because of my eighth-grade experience.

Then when I was a sophomore, I opened my heart to Sister John Francis in the guest dining room of that ancient academy. It was on an

October afternoon. Sunlight played through the lace curtains and made patterns on the table as we talked. "Entering is a fifty-fifty proposition. You have to accept the community and the community has to accept you," she stated matter-of-factly. That suited me. She didn't try to rope me in but left me free to decide. I responded joyfully inside. I could go on growing, living, and tasting God in my daily life. It was a good interview. I went away happy, expectant, challenged, and peaceful.

When I graduated from high school, my family felt that I needed to grow up before I entered the novitiate. "Go to college for at least a year" was their powerful advice. So I enrolled at Holy Names College in Spokane, Washington, where my brother Bill was going to Gonzaga on a scholarship. It was exciting to pack and to drive with Bill to Spokane in his newly acquired old Hudson car.

We drove through the barren wastelands of eastern Oregon and Washington states, and I was very impressed by the treeless terrain. It was so foreign to the green Willamette Valley of my youth. Its vastness seemed to swallow me up. I felt that God must be there to save me from that barren waste. The absence of trees made me feel very small.

At Holy Names College, I became friends with Sister Matilda Mary, who was head of the dramatics department. I took drama, and it almost killed me because I was so painfully shy. In one play, I had to be a French gendarme, wearing big boots, jeans, and a funny coat with a huge buckle. I had to stomp out and yell at some innocent children. It wasn't me at all. I remember thinking backstage while waiting to go on, *If I get through this play, I'll never sign up for drama class again.* I recall a sense of relief when it was all over. Sister Mattie May (as we nicknamed her) praised me for being fierce and for upholding the cast by keeping the action, which had lagged a bit, going. I remember the lovely sense of relief in letting go of my "me-ness" to be the policeman. After I learned how to relax, drama became more fun.

I dated boys and went to dances and movies. One tall, blond, handsome engineering student from Gonzaga took me out a number of times and wanted to kiss me at a movie. I said, "No," because I felt I belonged to Jesus and this was not for me. We could be friends, however, and I let Gene hold my hand at the movie. As I recall, Hamlet was never so exciting or meaningful as when we viewed it together.

I went home at Christmas and told my Mom about the dates, the boys, and Gene. She scolded me roundly and said, "Mary, you shouldn't lead that poor boy on when you don't intend to marry him."

"But Mom, you're the one who told me to go out with boys to know life! I only want to have a good time; I don't intend to marry. I still plan to be a nun, even more strongly than before."

When I returned to Spokane, I saw Gene again. I was honest with him, and he understood completely. We parted as friends, respecting each other but with the knowledge that we had to follow our individual calls. He wanted a wife and a family, and I wanted God more than ever. I knew certitude in those days—so I thought—that nothing could jolt.

In February, when the snow was still thick upon the city and the stately, majestic pines, my brother called me from Gonzaga and offered to take me for a ride around the city and then stop for lunch. We hadn't driven far when he came out with what had prompted his invitation.

"Now that you know a little more about life, do you still want to be a nun?" he asked.

"Yes, more than ever. The dances, the parties, the dates, and the movies are fun, but I need something much bigger. My heart was made for God, Bill. Nothing else will do."

"You're really convinced, aren't you?" he responded as he pulled up to the Three Hat Restaurant and parked the car.

"Yes, I am. You might say I am totally convinced." I looked at his eyes. They were very thoughtful as he took in my answer. I knew he had expected me to change, to let go of all the "vocation talk" and get lost in the college social world. I had no qualms about sharing with Bill; we were close.

I continued, "Marriage is fine, Bill, but it's not for me. Gene is a good fellow. I wish him luck; he deserves a good wife. I feel confident he will find the right partner."

Bill accepted where I was, and we enjoyed our lunch of toasted tuna melt sandwiches and Coke. Then we returned to our respective halls.

Sister Matilda Mary and I went for long walks in the snow and talked about things that were important to me, such as prayer and faith. I remember the day she pointed to the train smoke slowly rising and said, "Prayer is like that smoke; it goes gently to God." Deep-down-inside things were easy to share with her, and I felt very much at home, because God was real to her. She could scold Him or hug Him, depending on her mood.

Sister Mattie May's deep faith and genuineness before God were a great help to me. She was very direct, but her directness never hurt me, because I knew that she loved me and that she was perfectly honest. She was whole before God, and that helped me.

March came, and with it, enrollment for the third quarter. I enrolled in six classes, only to find that my mother wanted me to go home. I had planned to enter the novitiate on July 25th that summer. My mother felt that she was losing me and that I should forget about college and spend time with my family on the farm.

I was torn, because I could finish the quarter and still have a month and a half at home. I talked to Sister Matilda Mary and cried my eyes out. She listened and advised, "Do what your mother wants. You'll never regret it. There will be plenty of time to go to school."

I cried some more, and she patted my shoulder. She said, "You're always going to feel things. You are a sensitive person. You will have many highs and many lows." I look back fifty-two years later and realize how true this was.

At Loretto Hall, where I roomed with three other girls, I stayed in bed the following morning. Bertha, one of my roommates, asked, "Mary, are you sick?"

"No," I replied, "I'm skipping class."

All three of them giggled in surprise because this was so out of character. Betty insisted, "You must be sick."

"No," I replied, "I'm just going to take it easy." Playfully, I stuck my toes in the springs of the bunk above me. Seeing that they weren't going to budge me, they hurried off to class.

I lay in bed, mulling over my decision, still sadly considering the W's—withdrawals in six classes. I tried to think of the happiness it would bring my Mom, but I failed to convince myself. I did trust Sister Matilda Mary, and I knew that somehow everything would work out. Duty took over me as I mechanically got up and began packing for the long bus ride back to Oregon. I hated to leave the college I loved so well and the girls I was just beginning to know. With the psalmist, I said, "Like a weaver, you cut me off while I was yet beginning." I yearned for the lasting city—and it was not Spokane.

At home those last months, I tried to be very cheerful and helpful. My mother was very pleased that I had followed her wishes. At times, however, she got very emotional and threw her arms around me and said, "I'm losing you!"

"You're not really losing me, Mom. This is only a beginning."

I tried to calm her down, but my nineteen-year-old wisdom was not too effective. It made me sad to know my Mom felt sad, and I struggled to keep my own emotional peace. I thanked God at that time that my father didn't show his emotions so readily.

ENTRY

The day of my entry dawned. I wore a pretty, flowered, yellow cotton dress with princess lines, identical to the dress my little sister Zita had on. I couldn't see changing twice, so I wore the black stockings and low-heeled shoes I knew I'd be wearing once I got to Marylhurst, the place of our novitiate. It looked funny, but I didn't give a hoot.

On the way, we had a tasty picnic lunch with plenty of fried chicken. I ate some, but not heartily; excitement and nervousness killed my appetite. My father drove us some forty miles, from our home to Lake Oswego and then to Marylhurst. I remember the queasy feeling in my stomach as we rounded the rocky curve past the narrow bridge from Lake Oswego. I felt strained, but I didn't want anything to show. I felt as if I were jumping off a cliff into a vast unknown.

We arrived at the novitiate and were greeted by the provincial superior, Mother Joan, and some novices. A novice whisked me upstairs to change into my postulant dress.

I remember all the articles on the trousseau list, with all those yards of unbleached muslin and the size two-hundred thread. The man in the store where I bought the thread had remarked, "What are you going to do, mend a spider web?" I had no notion how to answer him because, at that time, I didn't realize we were going to mend the gauze on our coifs. I changed into the ankle-length postulant dress with the hot celluloid collar and black cape. I felt overdressed.

Next we went outside and joined the other postulants in the novitiate yard. Professed Sisters who knew us welcomed us with pleasant chatter. However, I remember Sister Erentrude, who had been my house mother at Loretto Hall in Spokane, looked at me in postulant attire and exclaimed, "My, the grace of God can do anything!"

I didn't feel too flattered, since I realized that some of my college pranks—such as throwing pillows after lights were out—had not set too well with Sister Erentrude. I hadn't warned her in any way that I was entering, and I knew that she was genuinely jolted because she didn't think I was the type. On the other hand, it made me secretly happy to know that I had thrown her off the trail.

We—the thirty-three postulants—were each given a novice to be our guardian angel, to guide us and to answer questions. My guardian angel was Sister Jerome Mary. She and I had both graduated from Sacred Heart Academy in Salem, but she had entered right out of high school while I had gone to college for almost a year.

She explained schedules and sleeping arrangements. She strongly advised not wearing a bra. "You won't want to; nobody wears one."

I thought to myself, *Like hell, I won't*, but I said nothing.

"See," she continued, "the waist of your dress fits tightly, and you don't need one."

"But," she added, seeing the alarm on my face, "you can wear one if you want to—but you will have to wash it yourself. You can't send it to the big laundry."

"That's okay. I'll wash it myself. No problem!" I replied, feeling very indignant, for I couldn't see a person of my size slopping around without a bra. My guardian angel was wise enough not to pursue the topic for a few days.

JESTEN — MILLER STUDIO

ad finem

High school graduation photo, 1949.

DANGLING

Nine o'clock came, and according to SNJM rules, it was time to retire, although on the evening of July 25, 1950, it was still fully daylight. I was in a dorm cell, situated on an aisle, next to Sister Georgia Maria, a professed Sister who helped in the novitiate. The cells were divided by heavy white curtains with cracks on the corners. Deploring the lack of privacy, I tried watching all four corners while getting undressed for bed. I felt like a nervous satellite doing the impossible. I was tense and jittery. Again I was that little five-year-old falling out of the haymow. That familiar dangling sensation in between the mow and the bottom was scary. The feeling of not knowing where I belonged was scary, too.

I stood there looking at the washbasin and pitcher. *Such an archaic system*, I thought. As I began nervously washing, I dropped the soap, and it slithered into the cell next to mine. The bony white hand of Sister Georgia Maria reached it back to me. I looked at that pale, skinny arm and thought, *Lord, she looks starved. Is this what religious life does? Do I belong here?*

I got into the tent-like muslin nightgown and longed for my pj's. I crawled under the white sheets and white bedspread and began earnestly conjecturing whether I should be in religious life. The answer I had so positively given for six years didn't seem that certain now. Through a crack in the curtain, I watched the sun go down. The sky got darker. Still I hadn't settled the crucial question. It got darker and darker. The darkness outside matched the indecision inside of me. Eventually the sky became gray. Finally the morning sun emerged, small and orange.

At 5:10 a.m., a loud rising bell sounded. I jumped up gladly. I hadn't slept all night, nor had I come to any decision; the night wasn't long enough. Turmoil reigned in my brain. I began the terrible process of getting dressed while watching all four corners of those moving, gaping curtains. The procedure was even more dreadful than the night before because I was so tired and drained.

Nevertheless, 5:45 a.m. found me in the chapel for morning prayer, followed by Mass at 6:30 a.m. and breakfast at 7:00 a.m., followed by a house charge. My eyes burned from the lack of sleep; yet, I tried to stay alert and keep my mind on the task at hand. That task was to clean a stairway with Betty, another postulant. It was rather fun, even though the rule said we had to keep silent. We learned the fine art of communicating without words.

Three days passed, and then we were whirled into an eight-day retreat. It was holy silence all day long and grand silence at night. (Grand silence was a strictly-observed time of reparation, during which no words were spoken, except in the rarest of emergencies.) I didn't really mind silence. We learned sign language to use at the table for salt and pepper and other articles of food. It was a novel way to eat.

Eight postulants returned to civilian life during our eight-day retreat. Their departure caused havoc inside me because I, too, was searching and struggling to know what my vocation was. "Lord, do I really belong here?" was in my heart and on my lips. I worked to come up with a hard and fast decision. None came.

Time went by, and my angel novice began pushing on the "you-won't-want-to-wear-a-bra" theme again. I felt distressed. Fortunately, at this point Sister Matilda Mary from Spokane visited me. She helped me to see that I didn't have to make up my mind right then as to whether or not I belonged. She patted my knee as we sat opposite each other, and she made me feel human. She listened to all the things I was hung up on. She said, "Don't hang yourself by a brassiere strap." And she chuckled in such a kind, friendly way when she said it, I couldn't help but laugh a little too. It made sense, but I was too undone to accept it totally. I was still fighting my indecision.

Again I was that little five-year-old dangling between the haymow and the bottom. Somehow I had to trust that God would land me safely. As yet, I didn't trust, and it hurt deeply. This struggle went on until October 3rd.

On the feast of St. Theresa, after much prayer, I got a powerful sense of belonging, and I never questioned my vocation again. It was real. I wasn't dangling any more; I had landed. Just as my Dad had picked me up out of the straw when I was a five-year-old, my heavenly Father picked me up and perched me on His knee—and that was that. Snug, safe, belonging forever and ever, I was His. God was calling me to this life. It was as clear as the sunshine and as real as the sticky chemise clinging to my warm body. On that October 3rd, I took a high-school graduation picture I had with me and wrote *Ad finem* on it. To the end, God would see me through.

A little later in October, as was customary, we postulants visited the provincial councilors. Sister Margherita, the provincial treasurer, greeted me and asked me how things were going. I replied that everything was fine; I was going to be a Holy Names Sister. I could see surprise written all over her. Her eyes got big and she replied quite briskly, "Well, we'll see about that."

I saw that she didn't share my conviction. In her mind, I was still on probation. Yet, in my heart, I never doubted. My belief was so strong; no councilor could shake it. I went away thinking, *She just doesn't understand.*

"Lord," I prayed, "You'll just have to explain it to her because I'm not fluent enough. To the end, You are going to see me through."

NOVITIATE DAYS

Days passed and the Christmas season came. We made wreaths and decorated every conceivable part of the novitiate. We wrote long letters home and decorated them with pictures cut from old Christmas cards. It was a fairly good indoor sport. We even wrote and produced little skits, which we performed for our novitiate friends. I remember the one I wrote called *The Christmas Donkey*. It was a play on words, and a postulant named Barbara Bray had to say the line, "And that made the donkey bray." It caused lots of laughs, and Sister Barbara still razzes me about that amateur performance.

As postulants, we weren't allowed to put our hair up or do anything considered worldly. My first novitiate haircut was a bowl cut. With my straight hair and round face, I looked awful. I wrote to my brother and said, "Got a haircut; looks like hell." Mother Gertrude censored the letter and gave it back to me to rewrite. Slang expressions were strictly forbidden; I had much to learn.

After the six months of postulancy, we became novices in February. At a very special Mass, we were called up into the sanctuary to receive our white veils. One of our tasks as postulants had been to sew our own veil. Now it was blessed and presented to us. We also received the holy habit with its yards and yards of pleated black serge. I remember how happy I felt on that February 5th in 1951. Wearing a coif, veil, and bandeau was a new experience, but in my heart, I was happy because these were symbols of belonging to God.

One assignment as novices was to write a vow paper on obedience. I called mine *Obedience, the Oblation of Love* and dedicated it to Mary, who would help me offer this perfect oblation to Jesus. We never got our papers back, so I only have the introduction, which I kept in my manuscript book.

> *It happened on a hill. Some call it a mountain, but it was really just a big hill. It was fitting that it should be big. Everything He did was big. The biggest sacrifice, the biggest obedience, the biggest love were His on the big hill of Calvary. Here He gave us the Mass, the perfect sacrifice, and I can give back to Him my Mass, the oblation of obedience, the offering of love to love.*

My cousin Agnes, who joined the Sisters of St. Mary shortly after I joined the Holy Names, wrote to me as often as the regulations permitted. We were more like sisters than cousins and compared everything. Aggie didn't like our headdress and told me bluntly in a letter. "Your horse blinders [meaning our coifs] really bug me."

Mother Gertrude dutifully read her letter and called me in with the strict admonition, "You must not let your cousin talk that way about our holy habit."

I listened carefully to her dissertation on the merits of the habit and then ventured, "Wouldn't it be more sensible to cut the gauze off so we can see better?"

At that suggestion, Mother Gertrude's face became red, and I thought her explosive reply would blow me not only out of her office but also right out of the community. I was soundly lectured on the sanctity of the habit.

Uniformity was stressed, and not being singular was a great virtue. We were given vow books to study for our vow class, and we were asked to cover them so they would stay clean for the next group of novices. All the novices around me used regulation brown paper. I chose pink paper that I managed to dig up in a drawer full of odds and ends. I lettered the title on my book in bold Chinese letters and felt very good about breaking the mass-production assembly-line technique.

Sister Kathleen, the oldest in our set, went to the mistress of novices and told her I was being singular. Mother Gertrude called me in and asked me for an explanation. I told her vehemently how unhealthy the evils of the American mass-production system were, where everything was made to look alike. I showed her my book with its bright cover and explained how I managed to escape the evil system that swallows people up and makes them unfree. She listened to me without getting angry, and I saw faint amusement in her deep blue eyes. She didn't make me use the ugly brown wrapping paper. I went away feeling one blow for freedom had been struck—and that I'd like to choke Sister Kathleen.

In the vow book, we were taught about various permissions: general, particular, expressed, presumed, tacit, licit, etc. To do anything, it was necessary to have permission. I listened carefully and decided it would be good to simplify the procedure, so I knocked on Mother Gertrude's door. She replied, "Come."

I went in and said, "May I please have a general permission?"

"A general permission to do what?"

"A general permission to do whatever is necessary," I replied in my youthful ignorance.

Her cheeks flamed. Her eyes spit fire. Her voice thundered, "You don't understand obedience at all. You have no concept of religious life. What am I going to do with you?"

"Well," I offered by way of explanation, "it would be a lot simpler than asking to go for a walk every time, or for a shoestring, or a bar of soap. A person would have time for more important things."

"Obedience *is* important!" she roared.

"All right, all right," I muttered, easing myself out while I was still in one piece. I was quite puzzled over the system because to my American-trained brain, it didn't make sense. Those books they read to us about planting cabbages upside down made better sense. Being from a farm, I knew that cabbages were smart enough to right themselves and grow straight. "But," I asked myself, "would people trained in this fashion right themselves? Would they grow straight in God, or would they get all hung up in all sorts of trivia?" I asked God to help me to understand and to soothe Mother Gertrude. I knew it wasn't good for her to get so angry, and I didn't feel that it did me any particular good, either.

My brother Bill had always said in high-school days, "The knocks of life either make you or break you." I was determined to grow through all the hard things, so I made a short prayer to fit these rough times. "Thank You, God, for all the ouches of today." It was a very handy prayer. I wore that prayer out in the novitiate.

We, the postulants and novices, had picnics down by the Willamette River on our property in a place called "The Rocks." One summer evening, we were having a picnic there, and my friend, Sister Karen Rose, a novice, had to leave early to do her chores in the diet kitchen. We were supposed to have toasted marshmallows at the end of the picnic supper.

"Oh heck," she said, "I'll miss the marshmallows."

"Don't worry; I'll save you some," I said.

"But they won't be toasted."

"Have no fear; I'll see to that too," I replied. She gave me a quizzical look and left. I wrapped up a goodly supply of marshmallows and stuffed them in my pockets. We had pockets so ample you could carry a good-sized book in them without bulge or embarrassment.

Due to the huge numbers in our novitiate, Sister Karen Rose and I slept in one of the towers above the dorm. Mother Gertrude slept in the opposite tower. This sleeping arrangement furthered my plan for the marshmallows.

After we got back to the novitiate, I got a vigil light from Mater Admirabile's shrine, some matches, and some wooden applicators, which were used with cotton balls to check ears. These I took to our tower, and then in grand silence, without a word, I proceeded to toast the marshmallows, first being careful to throw a blanket over the stairway so that the dancing flame wouldn't disturb the novices below. We quietly enjoyed the marshmallows, and then, at recreation the next day, we shared the event with Sister Ann Monica. Sister had a fine sense of humor and quoted a line from our office book, "And there shall be plenteousness in their towers."

We quoted that line every time things got rough, although our companions couldn't understand why "plenteousness in their towers" should cause such hilarity. We couldn't explain; it was too risky.

Tricks in the dorm were heavily frowned upon. Occasionally, someone would try some little thing. Once when I was sleeping next to Sister Barbara Bray, who had a sacristy charge and could never get upstairs on time to get herself ready for bed, I turned down her bed covers and put out her nightgown, slippers, and nightcap. That night as I set them out, I noticed how the floor tiles were all very dark mottled brown. I set her slippers by the bed, tied dark thread to each one, and unwound the spool under her bed into my cell. I made haste and brushed my teeth and got into bed, being careful to peer under her bed and mine to see when she would reach for her slippers. As her hand came down for the first one, I gently tweaked it away. She let out a breathless squeal and reached for the other one. It jumped away from her. She laughed—as only Sister Barbara can—when she discovered me on the other end. We both laughed guardedly, just a few chuckles, because Mother Gertrude's tower was in close proximity and we didn't want any trouble.

Our first novice's retreat was better than our postulant retreat. There was less hellfire and more love of God. In that retreat, I wrote:

> *Jesus, You are my ideal. Teach me how to love You better. The rules of this institute are a rainbow fanned out of love of God. Love is all that matters....*

The days ahead were busy and happy with plenty of ups and downs. We canned applesauce and sewed coifs. We prayed, recreated, and went for long hikes. We sat in the tall grass outside the novitiate and grumbled about how awful it was not to have clean linens on our beds every week. The bedsheet system was so very unsanitary—truly, it was a medieval mentality. Those in charge didn't seem concerned that we'd die of germs—and we didn't. A Sister who was one year ahead of me deplored the bath system with a schedule that allowed only ten minutes per person. "Kill me; shoot me; do anything to me, but don't take my bath time," Sister Marion Lawrence would say. Somehow we all survived.

NURSING EXPERIENCE

After first vows, I was scheduled to go to Spokane to study in preparation for teaching. Two weeks before I was to go on the train, Sister Dorothy Ann of the Provincial Council called me into her office.

"Sister, won't you please sit down?"

My head was in a whirl. I thought, *Who could have died in my family?*

She continued, "We are short of helpers in the infirmary, and we thought you would be good up there. Are you willing to give one year to help care for the sick?"

"Yes," I replied, somewhat startled. "But I don't know anything about nursing."

"Oh, don't worry about that; Sister Annette Marie and Sister Claudiana are both RNs. They will teach you."

"All right," I said, relieved that no one in my family had died. One year of service wasn't anything so forbidding.

I began learning practical nursing. I practiced giving shots on oranges before doing them on live people. I was shown many routine procedures, such as how to give a bed bath, how to turn a patient, and how to insert a feeding tube.

I had six patients. Three of these were very sick and three were ambulatory. Sister Hyacintha was my patient needing the most care. A stroke had paralyzed her on one side. Sister Gertrude Frances was a heart patient, able to walk a little. Sister Elmire was very French, very sweet, and very elderly, suffering from palsy and old age. I liked her a lot. She was very, very prayerful, and peace radiated from her. Sister Margaret Maureen had back surgery and was making a good recovery. I can't remember the other two patients.

Sister Marion Lawrence's patient, Sister Florence Agatha, had a stroke that didn't paralyze her but put her out of touch with reality. She did odd things and was very anti-social. I remember being asked one day to help her to eat. As I coaxed her to eat some boiled carrots, she became very angry. Her faded blue eyes flashed fire, and she threw the fork at me. I ducked, and it went sailing across the room. I went out and told the head nurse how dangerous it was to feed her, and the head nurse let me off.

When I began working in the infirmary, Sister Margherita, who had been our provincial treasurer, was dying of cancer. I didn't like the idea of anyone dying, so I took off to Rosecliffe, one of the residential halls on the campus, to escape. I came back after she died and quietly resumed my work. No one even missed me. It was the big feast of Our Lady's Assumption on August 15, 1952.

Several more patients died in the next few months. I didn't like it at all. Mother Joan came up to the infirmary and asked me how I liked working there.

"Oh Mother," I blurted out, "I don't mind the work, but I belong in the land of the living."

She cheered me up by telling me how much the sick appreciated me. In December when Sister Florence Agatha had died, I had told a fellow nurse that if any of my patients died, I would die too. She told me not to talk that way. "I can't help it; that's the way I feel," I replied.

January came, and Sister Hyacintha, who fondly called me "Teddy Bear," took a turn for the worse. On January 24th, the head nurse said she would be anointed because she was going to die.

"No," I said, "She can't die. I won't let her die!"

Sister Claudiana shook her head, turned to me, and replied, "Lambie, it can't be stopped. Her kidneys are failing. There is nothing we can do." I continued stuffing applesauce, her favorite food, into her, somehow convinced that this would save her.

Father Carroll, our chaplain, was very devoted to the sick. He came to anoint her. Her right side was not paralyzed; she had plenty of zip on that side. She hated anyone to touch her face. In washing her face, I had to go very carefully, or she would hit me. Father Carroll didn't know that. He anointed her eyelids—and she hauled off and slapped him soundly on the cheek.

Mother Joan, Provincial Superior, got red with embarrassment and instructed Sister Victor Mary and me to hold her hand. We were both struggling to keep from laughing out loud. Father was not upset; he understood Sister and loved her. I kept thinking, "Three cheers! If you can whack the chaplain, you are not about to die. Anyone with that much vigor is not about to go to God." I was secretly satisfied that the RN had made a big mistake.

I went about the business of taking care of her and feeding her more applesauce. Sister Claudiana looked at me with her friendly smile and in a gentle way said, "Applesauce won't save her."

I didn't reply, because I didn't want to believe her. Sister Dorothy Ann came upstairs to visit Sister Hyacintha and went away disgusted because she was more interested in eating her applesauce than in visiting.

Three days later, she got very bad. Her breathing was labored; her kidneys were failing. Sisters sat with her day and night. I wore myself out trying to keep her alive. I still didn't want to believe that the end was inevitable. On January 27th at 10:00 a.m., I stood by her bed holding her hand and praying as she took one deep breath, let it out, and stopped breathing. She was dead.

I cried. Mother Joan put her arms around me and hugged me. I cried some more—I flooded the place. Then Sister Celeste Marie, a friend in our set, said, "Let's go for a walk."

Sister Victor Mary scolded me, saying, "You shouldn't cry; it's selfish to cry. She lived a long life. She wanted to be with God. Let her go." My only answer was to sob even louder. My "Teddy Bear" was gone, and I couldn't quite let go.

Sister Celeste Marie had the right idea. We walked and talked. Gradually I let go a little bit, and it didn't hurt so badly. It wasn't that I didn't want her to go to God. It was just the awful reality of death that was too much for me to handle at twenty-one years of age. In February and March, more Sisters died. After losing my own patient, I was in better shape to let go of the others—but it was still hard.

I remember the directions given me, when I first worked in the infirmary, on how to give a backrub:

"Put on the lotion, put on the talcum powder, and rub until they disappear." It all sounded so simple.

My first victim was Sister Gertrude Frances. She was a heart patient, outgoing, vivacious, happy, and enthusiastic. She said nothing as I generously poured on lotion and talcum powder and proceeded to rub vigorously.

The only trouble was that it didn't disappear. I tried harder, with no luck. Finally, after the pasty mess just got more gluelike and didn't disappear at all, she thanked me and said I could go. Relieved, I left. She hurried out and took a shower. I went back to Sister Claudiana and protested that her directions didn't work. She listened and then laughed so hard I thought she'd never stop. She repeated her directions:

"Put the lotion on and rub it until it disappears; *then* put a little talcum on."

We laughed together, and Sister Gertrude Frances laughed too.

FIRST YEAR TEACHING

After one year working as a nurse, I went back to College at Marylhurst, and then to Spokane to do my practice teaching. I taught at St. Aloysius in the third grade with Sister Roberta Ann. She was a nervous wreck, because the doctor had given her the wrong medicine for a thyroid condition, which resulted in her getting more high-strung and nervous as the semester continued on. By the middle of March, she was too sick to continue, and the responsibility for all fifty-six third-graders fell into my lap. I felt a bit overwhelmed, but I was glad to have Sister Lavone, who was teaching the other third grade across from me, as co-helper. (This school had a double room of each grade.)

The principal, Sister Evelyn Mary, was helpful too. I remember her telling me that, if the class got out of hand, all I needed to do was to send her a note with an X on it and she would come to my rescue. I was never in such desperate shape that I sent her any X notes.

But I did have some discipline problems. The staff was more experienced than I, so I listened to various remedies for misbehavior. One teacher said to have the naughty pupil stand and look into the wastebasket. She claimed this was a sure cure. I tried it once. It struck me as so ridiculous that I couldn't keep a straight face. I ended up sending the child back to his desk and tossing out that method for good.

Dennis was a terrible problem. He was small, blond, immature, and unable to cope with third-grade work. He was constantly interrupting. I tried everything I knew with him, but nothing seemed to work. The wastebasket method was utterly useless, as he didn't mind wasting time.

I was told that another acceptable disciplinary measure was to shake the culprit. One day when Dennis was constantly chattering, I went over to his desk, informed him that he was causing a disturbance, took him by the shoulders, and shook the little guy. He was so tiny that I swung him off his feet and he went back and forth like a swing in motion. The effect was electrifying on the rest of the class. They all behaved exceptionally well for the rest of that day. As for Dennis, it didn't really cure him. What he really needed was work he could handle, and I was too inexperienced to meet his individual needs.

And then there was Freddie. He was large boned, dark, slow to comprehend, hating every minute of school, always looking for distractions, and creating them whenever he could. He sat by a radiator, the old-fashioned kind that released a whirl of hot air every twenty minutes or so, on a regular cycle. Freddie designed a parachute, with a big red bandana knotted through three holes in a ruler. He sent it up in the radiator's updraft. This kept him and his friends conveniently entertained. As soon as I began the first reading group, up went the parachute. Frustrated, I confiscated the ruler and the red bandana—no more parachute. Freddie looked sad, but he knew his parachuting days were ended.

After Sister Evelyn Mary left St. Aloysius, Sister Kathleen Clare came to be principal and superior. She was a tall redhead—quiet, efficient, and kind. I liked her. I didn't always agree with her, but I still liked her. She was firm with Sisters who were unorganized or slovenly in their ways.

Sister Susan Ann was such a person—unorganized, never on time, always in trouble—but a lovable second-grade teacher. I cannot remember a time when she was *not* in trouble. Because she felt like she did not have time to mend the holes in the heels of her black stockings, she pinned them shut with safety pins. Sister Superior took her to task for that; it was not according to the rubrics!

I remember one time when Sister Susan got a horrible cold and Sister Doreen was the infirmarian. Sister Doreen brought her some hot lemonade, which Sister Susan only partially drank. Then the superior came along and scolded her for not drinking the whole glass. She sternly admonished her to take all the meds provided.

The next evening, the superior told Sister Doreen to give Sister Susan a hot toddy. Sister Doreen was not knowledgeable about such things, so she filled a beer stein half full of whiskey, poured the other half full of boiling water, and presented it to Sister Susan. She gulped and drank it all, in view of the sound dressing down she had received earlier from the superior.

Not too long after this, Sister Susan started laughing and could not stop. Then she had to go to the bathroom. When she got up, she couldn't walk straight, but with a little help, she managed to get there. Fortunately the cold was cured overnight, and her temperature returned to normal. (Sister

Lavone and I both took time to instruct Sister Doreen in the art of toddy making.)

The next year, Sister Lavone and I were appointed infirmarians. Sister Kathleen Clare was prone to migraines. I remember one Saturday when she was in bed with one and Sister Lavone, in an effort to relieve the soreness in her neck, rubbed in some strong liniment. When I went in at 10:00 to bring her hot tea, she was in such misery and her neck was so red, it outdid her red hair. She asked, "Could you help me get this horse liniment off?"

I washed her neck, and it got better gradually. Sister Lavone, who is very kind-hearted, was sad to know that the liniment didn't work. "Redheads' skin is too delicate for that," she concluded.

AS BIG AS A FOOTBALL

As the school year progressed, I kept getting a pain in my back, and my monthly periods extended to nine or ten days. I told the superior, Sister Ann Clare, who said it wasn't serious. She said that I was just eating too much applesauce. I persisted in complaining, and she sent me to a foot doctor. (I did have bad feet.) Sister Ann Clare said that my feet were probably affecting my back. The podiatrist fixed new shoe appliances, which didn't change the pain in my back. It got progressively worse.

From December until March, walking, sitting, and lying down were miserable for me. I tried various remedies, even sleeping on a board, which didn't help. Finally the superior sent me to another doctor, who took x-rays of my back. A day later the doctor's nurse phoned and insisted that I come in immediately.

The doctor came to the point right away. "Your x-ray shows that you have a large tumor in your abdomen. It is as big as a football, about the size of a mother who is six months pregnant."

"That's not my x-ray," I stated boldly as a rash broke out across my neck and chest.

"Yes, this is your x-ray," the doctor said firmly and gently, "and we'll have to do surgery immediately. Plan it for Monday."

"But this can't be!" I sputtered.

"But it is, and the only good thing about it is that a tumor this size can't be cancer. If it were cancer, you'd be dead."

On that cheery note, I left. Badly shaken, I went back to the convent to tell Sister Ann Clare. I had never had surgery in my life, not even my tonsils out.

I stepped into Sister Ann Clare's office and started crying.

"Sit down and tell me about it," she said kindly.

I pulled the door shut and proceeded to relate all that the doctor had said. She listened attentively and tried to cheer me up. Then she teased me about flooding the floor with tears and said she'd have to mop it. I felt better after I got the whole report out. Then Sister Ann Clare informed me of all the pre-surgery steps the hospital would take, such as blood tests and hypos. I listened carefully.

I packed my bag, being careful to include my office book, a small statue of Mary, and a holy card, which Sister Ann Clare had given to me, with this Francis Thompson quote: "All that I did take from thee, I did take not for thy harms, but just that you might seek it in my arms."

Sister Doris Ellen, who was the house driver, drove me to the hospital, along with Sister Ann Clare. The Providence Sister, who did the admitting, looked at Sister Doris Ellen, who was always pale, and asked, "Are you the patient?"

"No," she laughed.

Next the admitting Sister tried Sister Ann Clare, who was prone to migraines.

"I'm not the one," smiled Sister Ann Clare.

Finally she turned to me (pink cheeked and healthy looking). Then we all laughed, because it was a little funny.

They settled me in my room, and as soon as they left, I started arranging my few items. After I said my office, I planted the holy card under the glass top on the bureau and put the statue of Mary where I could see it.

The next morning, I got up and went to the early Mass. After Mass, I crawled back into bed until the nurses prepared me for 9:00 a.m. surgery. One nurse came in and gave me a hypo in the hip. This made me feel very relaxed, as if I were floating. Then two nurses put me on a stretcher and started to take me up the elevator to the surgery floor. I felt so totally peaceful that they could have cut my head off and I wouldn't have protested.

Then I remembered and said to the nurse, "Hey, you didn't take a blood test."

She looked startled, fumbled through the charts, and said to the other nurse, "She's right; there is no blood test here. We'll have to take her back and do it. The doctor will be furious."

After the blood test was completed, they took me to the surgery room. The lights were harsh and glaring. One nurse put a piece of cotton between my thumb and first finger and said, "Now hold that as long as you can." It was a neat trick to see when the anesthetic took effect on me.

Four hours later, in the recovery room, I turned to the nurse and asked, "Can I let go of the cotton now?"

"What cotton?"

"The cotton you told me to hold," I said evenly.

They thought that I was out of my head. However, they had removed a tumor as large as a football. A little later when I opened my eyes in my own room, I was glad to see Sister Ann Clare.

"What time is it?" I asked.

"Two o'clock," she replied.

"How many holes are in my middle?"

"One," she replied.

"Good," I said, satisfied that they hadn't done any unnecessary cutting. I sank back into my pillows. She urged me to rest and said she would keep on praying for my recovery. I slept.

The next day, my brother George and his wife Elaine came to see me. My brother Bill brought me an orchid. It was gorgeous. I admired it on my tray table.

After my family left, the nurse came in and asked if I was hungry. I said, "Yes." She brought me a dish of red jello and a spoon, then rolled the bed up and asked if I wanted her to feed me.

"No," I replied, "I can feed myself."

She left. I looked at the jello. It looked good, and I reached for the spoon. It was awful heavy. I set it down and thought, " I'll sleep first and eat it later." I closed my eyes and promptly went to sleep. When I woke six hours later, the red jello and the spoon were gone. I was angry that someone had swiped my jello, but I was too tired to protest.

My surgeon, Dr. Penna, came in and examined my incision. He said that it would be painful for a while but I was doing well. Then he read the holy card under the glass and broke out in loud guffaws. I didn't know what was so funny until he read it to me.

"All that I did take from thee, I did take not for thy harms but just that you might seek it in my arms."

He laughed some more. I smiled weakly; it was too painful to laugh. He left.

I was cold—there were never enough blankets. I put my bathrobe on my bed in an effort to get warm. I rang for more blankets, but they never came.

After a week in the hospital, I spent two weeks at the convent before I returned to my fifth-grade classroom. I found that I could manage fairly well if I had a little help with closing and opening the heavy windows.

CHRISTMAS AT SAINT ALOYSIUS

Summer came and went. Fall found me teaching the fifth grade again. Time moved on, and we all received Christmas charges. Mine was to help Sister Cordelia put up a Christmas tree in the front parlor. Because Sister Cordelia was the oldest Sister in the house, she had the parlor for a charge.

Two weeks earlier, at a house meeting, Sister Ann Clare had asked us if we needed any lights, tinsel, extension cords, or decorations. She said, "Speak up now, or hold your peace forever." I didn't speak up, because I wasn't aware of needing anything, nor was I in charge.

As I helped Sister Cordelia the afternoon of December 24, she said, "We need an extension cord, because this one won't reach. Go, ask Sister Superior if you may borrow one from school."

I knocked timidly on Sister Ann Clare's door. "May I get an extension cord from school for Sister Cordelia? Hers won't reach."

"No," she thundered, "I told you Sisters two weeks ago to take care of all your Christmas needs. We are not borrowing anything from school—and that's final!"

I left, feeling hurt, and reported back to Sister Cordelia. She shrugged but didn't seem too upset. Then I went to my room, feeling abused because Sister Superior had yelled at me. I sat down listlessly and began wrapping small packages, slapping the paper on and thinking how unfair it was. *Why did she yell at me? I was only trying to help that old nun.*

A knock came on my door.

"Yes," I called out.

It was Sister Ann Clare. "I'm sorry I was so icky about that extension cord. Go ahead and get one from school so Sister Cordelia can finish her tree."

"Thank you," I said and forgave her on the spot. My heart was singing as I rushed to get the cord and finish the tree.

HYPO EXPERIENCE

Christmas came and went. Spring arrived, and with it came trouble. Our sixth-grade teacher, Sister Marian Rose, was very sports minded. One sunny March day during the noon hour, she played football with her sixth-grade boys and landed on her knee. Rather than tell anyone, she tried teaching that afternoon from a sitting position. As the afternoon dragged on, the knee swelled up with so much pain that Sister Marian Rose thought she would faint. At that point, she sent for Sister Ann Clare, who had to call an ambulance to take her to the hospital.

Emergency-room doctors fixed her up and prescribed shots every four hours for the pain, if needed. She could not walk up the stairs, so she was given a bell to ring for assistance. Sister Ann Clare slept above her and assured Sister that she would help her during the night.

"But," she pointed out, "I cannot give you a shot."

"Don't worry," I replied. "Just come wake me up, and I'll give whatever shots are needed. I'll load the shot before I go to bed."

In those days, it was grand silence from 9:00 p.m. until after Mass the following morning. No words were spoken, except in the rarest emergency. I went peacefully to bed and slept as I usually do—dead to the world.

In the middle of the night, Sister Ann Clare came to wake me. She shook the bed—no response. She shook me—no response. Finally, she pulled me to a sitting position and said in my ear, "Hypo!"

All my sleepy brain heard was, "hi ho" and I thought, "What a funny greeting in the middle of the night."

But she kept it up. "Hypo!"

"Hi ho," my brain translated. I wasn't the Lone Ranger; what did this mean? Again, I slumped back onto the bed.

Finally Sister Ann Clare shook me sufficiently awake for me to register and give the injection.

TEACHING FIFTH GRADE

My experience teaching the fifth grade was much more encouraging than my teaching of the third grade. Classes were still huge, at least fifty students, but fifth-graders were much more capable and I understood them better.

I remember Sunshine Mugill, a sandy-haired boy from the orphanage. Some of the girls reported that he had a live mouse in his pocket. I marched down the aisle in the middle of a penmanship class, thrust out my hand, and demanded, "Give me that mouse."

Startled, Sunshine fumbled in his pocket and pulled out a very limp, dead mouse. I wrapped it neatly in a paper towel, put it carefully in the wastebasket, and washed my hands thoroughly. Then I lectured the class on how unsanitary it is to handle mice.

One boy observed, "You're not afraid of them, are you, Sister?"

"No," I replied, "but I don't like them around, because of the germs they carry." That concluded the mice for that year.

From Spokane, I went to Marylhurst. There, on August 5, 1957, I made my final vows with twenty-six other young Sisters. Wild sweet peas of deep magenta decorated our vow candles. The small chapel was crowded; only relatives with tickets could attend. It was a hot, happy day. Words from the ceremony hung in my head, "espoused to Him whom the sun and moon obey." I felt peace, even though I was excited.

I remember walking back to my chapel place and smiling at my cousin on the way. I remember the feel of the gold ring on my finger. *His forever*. I remember touching my profession crucifix, the symbol of fidelity and service. Although we were crowded eight in a pew, and Sister Mary Paul teased us about having to take turns breathing, I didn't mind. Joy colored that day, and no small discomfort could dim it. What I had so longed for—final profession—was finally realized after seven long years.

After final vows, I visited my family for a day. Since the rule required that a Sister have a companion, Sister Celeste Marie accompanied me. For the big family dinner, Mother used a linen tablecloth and linen napkins. Sister Celeste Marie complimented her on the beautiful cloth, and that simple word of appreciation relaxed me, because I had felt a little nervous, wondering if Sister would like my family.

After teaching in Spokane, I was transferred to St. Mary's in Seattle, which was a very poor parish of mixed races: African American, Filipino, Chinese, Japanese, Italian, Polish, and Caucasian. I taught forty-five fifth graders in a crowded second-story classroom. Of these forty-five, George Frangello was a challenge—active, dark haired, exuberant, intelligent, undisciplined—he never missed a chance to test my skill.

Since our coat hall was so crowded and small, I parked my size-twelve rubbers under my desk. One recess, George pulled one out and proceeded to stick both of his feet into it, observing with a grin, "Look, two of mine will fit into one of yours."

"Yes, mine are Longfellows," I agreed.

George noticed how I picked up the back of my skirt when walking down the stairs, and inquired most politely, "Sister, could I carry your train for you?"

I thanked him, and assured him that I could manage it.

MY BONES BELONG TO ME

Before I entered, I had serious foot problems, having inherited a bone-structure problem from my mom. While in the novitiate, I was sent to a foot doctor who massaged my feet and talked incessantly of balancing my inlays. But he never did. I got weary and stopped going to him.

In Seattle, my new superior, Sister Angela Felice, was a fanatic on health and insisted that I go to a "good, Catholic foot doctor." (Why a foot doctor had to be Catholic to be good, I could never see.) But, obediently, I went to the doctor of her choice.

After five months of incompetent service, he proposed bone surgery on my feet during the Christmas vacation. He planned to take out an inch of bone from each toe and promised me I would recover fully during the two weeks of vacation. From my short experience working with sick and surgery patients, I knew that foot-bone surgeries didn't recover that fast. When I told the superior what the doctor proposed, she was all for it. I told her flatly that I didn't want surgery and I didn't want my bones cut out. The more I protested, the more she insisted I had to have it done.

"Your health belongs to the community," she said.

"My bones belong to me," I countered.

We argued—and got nowhere. Fortunately, Sister Dorothy Ann, Provincial Assistant, came for her annual visit. I was never more delighted to see an official visitor. When it came my turn to see her, I rushed in and blurted out, "I don't want my bones cut out—I need them!"

Sister Dorothy Ann looked at me in alarm and said very cordially, "Sister, do sit down and tell me about this from the beginning." So I did.

She understood perfectly and arranged with that superior that I didn't even have to go back to that doctor. I thanked God that day, and many days after, that my toe bones are still intact.

AIRPLANE MANIA

The next year, I taught the sixth grade in that same school. We had a unit in science on airplanes. One student's father flew small planes in Seattle. This sixth-grader, Patrick Pomeroy, naturally was vitally interested in airplanes. Since the whole class showed interest too, I began to set up a field trip to the nearest airport.

Patrick was enthusiastic and asked me, "Sister, have you ever been up in an airplane?"

"No, I haven't."

"Would you like to?"

"Yes, but it's out of the question. I'd have to see Mother Provincial and get her permission. We just don't do things like that unless there is a very serious reason. So forget it, Patrick."

But Patrick didn't forget it. "Who is the Mother Provincial?"

"Mother Mark."

"Where does she live?"

"In Oregon, at Marylhurst, far from here," I

replied, satisfied that this airplane flight was settled.

Patrick came back the next morning all aglow and announced, "My Dad called Mother Provincial. You have permission to go up in an airplane."

"Oh, no," I groaned, and under my breath added, "You just don't do things like this." Aloud I faltered, "Thank your Dad, for me," and to myself I worried how I would ever explain this to a superior who was already on strained terms with me. That evening I went into her office and bravely attempted an explanation.

She accused me of putting Patrick up to it.

"But, I didn't," I replied. "All I said was that I like airplanes. It was his idea."

"Sure, sure, blame it all on an eleven-year-old," she scolded. Then she turned angrily to me. "You write and explain this to Mother Provincial."

"All right, I will," I said, confident that my ability to express it on paper far exceeded my ability to speak. I went to my room, sat down, and wrote eleven pages to Mother Mark.

In those days, we had no money and no stamps for our personal use. I went to the cupboard where the stamps for letters to Mother Provincial were supposed to be kept, but there were none. I took my sealed letter to Sister Angela Felice, the superior, and asked her to mail it, explaining that there were no stamps. Angrily, she grabbed the letter out of my hand, flung it across the desk, and yelled, "I'll mail it if I feel like it!"

I watched with horror as my letter skidded across the glass of her desk and slipped between the desk and wall. She didn't retrieve it in my presence. I left with the horrible feeling that I might have to write that letter again.

The next day was Ascension Thursday, which meant no school. At breakfast that morning, we were each given twenty-five cents to spend at the church carnival. I didn't spend mine; I saved it in case I needed to buy stamps, which only cost three cents at that time.

The convent where we lived was a remodeled house. The front phone booth had old-fashioned glass doors. Two days after that horrible letter episode, the phone rang early in the morning. I knew it was Mother Mark by the way Sister turned her back when she answered the phone. I went upstairs to put the sacristy in order and the vestments away. Another Sister came and told me I was wanted on the phone.

It was Mother Mark. "Sister, I was so glad to get your letter. If I hadn't gotten your letter, I would never have understood this airplane situation."

I literally hugged her through the phone. "Oh, I'm so glad you understand. Thank you." The relief in my voice was real.

She didn't have to say anything more. The long vigil was ended. I didn't even have to buy a stamp! I said, "Thank You, God, for taking care of this. I am grateful."

HYPOCHONDRIAC

At times, this same superior was almost irrational about health problems. She appointed herself house infirmarian and loved doling out pills, cough syrups, ointments, and any other medicine she felt was good for us. Sometimes we rebelled.

One fall, my friend Sister James Thomas and I caught bad colds, which persisted for weeks because we never took care of them. Sister Angela Felice fussed a great deal about these colds and actually sent us to a doctor for a checkup. We didn't want to go, but we had no choice. The doctor was friendly, and he didn't do anything more radical than prescribing cough syrup. Sister James Thomas's cold went away, but mine didn't, perhaps because I never got to bed very early.

The fact that my cold stayed on infuriated Sister Angela Felice. She made me stay in bed one Saturday and called her brother, a doctor.

In those days, we wore tent-like muslin nightgowns with rubber buttons, so they could go through the mangle. Those buttons I hated with a passion, because they never stayed shut in the front. So I solved that problem by sewing my nightgown down the front, leaving only an opening big enough to slip my head through.

The doctor came, and Sister Angela Felice wanted him to examine my chest. She tried to unbutton my nightgown but failed. Angrily she whipped out her scissors and, for an awful second, I thought that she was going to run me through. She proceeded to cut out all my sewing as the doctor questioned, "How do you feel?"

"Fine," I replied.

Sister Angela Felice glared at me. (She wanted me to say I was dying—but I wasn't.) The doctor took that in, but he didn't let on. Smiling, he prescribed more cough syrup and departed. After they were gone, I laughed. It was funny.

WISDOM TEETH

Small household regulations were very sacred to Sister Angela Felice. She became very nervous and uptight if schedules were not followed to the second. For example, she insisted that every Sister be present on Fridays at 4:00 p.m. when the priest arrived to hear confessions. Knowing this, I very dutifully made my dentist appointments for a Wednesday or Thursday afternoon. I had two impacted wisdom teeth that needed extracting.

Sister Angela Felice insisted on being my companion. Unfortunately, I was wearing my best holy habit, because I had taken my daily one apart to wash it. The dentistry was difficult. He had to work hard to pull those teeth.

"Would you like to keep the teeth?" the dentist asked, preparing to put them in a small envelope.

"Yes," I replied, being curious about wisdom teeth.

"No; heavens, no!" Sister Angela Felice cut in with such a vehement tone that the dentist looked from me to her and hesitated. I still wanted them, but she kept voicing such disapproval that the dentist shrugged and tossed them out.

Then, when I felt sick to my stomach because of the anesthetic, the superior told the nurse to give me some tea. I tried to explain that tea would only further unsettle me, knowing this from my hospital experience. However, Sister Angela Felice wouldn't listen. She demanded even more firmly that the nurse bring me some tea.

The nurse obliged. I drank a little, hoping to get by with a sip or two. But it didn't work. Sister Angela Felice kept fussing until the whole cup was finished.

We started home in a taxi, because we didn't have cars in those days. I felt miserable. My head was pounding, and my stomach churned uneasily. Halfway home, I vomited tea and blood all over my good holy habit.

Angry and embarrassed, Sister Angela Felice exclaimed, "Don't do that!"

Disgusted, I made no reply, although I wanted say, "Who the hell throws up on purpose?"

I resented the fact that she violated my personhood by making me drink tea and not allowing me to inspect my own wisdom teeth. I lacked the tools to know how to insist on my own rights, and that distressed me. Even though I had committed my life to God, my bones and my teeth still belonged to me. Inside, I argued, *God wouldn't act that way; why does she?*

There was no answer. I was too young to understand. I had to live through a lot more pain before I realized that there are many events in life that are totally irrational and that I needed God's healing touch if I was ever going to be whole. That would come much later, when I finally managed to forgive Sister Angela Felice.

Not long after this, Sister James Thomas and I were downtown shopping on a very windy, rainy Saturday afternoon. With our arms full of packages and our voluminous mantles catching the heavy wind like kites, we were crossing a busy intersection when my mantle broke loose from under my arm and neatly wrapped itself, like a cocoon, around a fellow pedestrian.

We kept walking; there was nothing else to do. When we got across the street, we unwrapped him. It was like, "Lazarus, come forth." And he looked more surprised, I think, than Lazarus had.

There was much that was good and beautiful at St. Mary's. I loved the students. Their variety was infinite. One time, a Japanese family invited us to dinner at their home. We went and enjoyed deliciously prepared fish, seaweed cookies, and delicate vegetables. We laughed later because Sister Lillian didn't like the seaweed cookies, and not wishing to offend her most polite hostesses, she slipped the unwanted cookie into her large pocket where no one would ever know if she ate it or not.

The next year, I was transferred to Portland, where I taught at St. Philip Neri School. Sister Bernadette Mary was a lovely superior and a remarkable principal. She was kind and firm. We got along very well. She helped me in teaching the seventh grade, which was new to me.

WHITE GUARDRAILS

While I was teaching at Saint Philip Neri, seven of us—out of a possible ten—agreed to go to a seminary play at Mount Angel, two weeks before Easter.

As our station wagon zipped along the freeway at seventy miles per hour (the speed limit at that time), we disagreed on where the cut off was for Mount Angel. Suddenly we came upon it, and Sister Bernadette Mary, our driver, turned off sharply, still going at the freeway speed. I noted the sign reading forty-five miles per hour and winced. She hadn't seen it.

The next sign said, "Prepare to stop." She didn't see that sign, either. Tension mounted inside me. All I could think was, *I don't want to die. I don't want to go through that windshield. What if we land upside down on the freeway below the overpass? Stop! Please stop, Bernadette.*

But we didn't stop. We smashed into the guardrail. "Here we go," Sister Mary Phyllis said in a still, small voice as the back end of the car went up.

I braced myself and thought, *I don't want to go through that windshield*. I pushed so hard that I ended up with a bruise as big as a saucer on my leg. The car was standing on its two front wheels. I thought that the pavement was going to hit me in the face. I wanted to yell.

The back end of the car came down, but we kept turning and came to a shuddering stop in the middle of the overpass.

I glanced at Sister Bernadette Mary, who was ashen. She stammered, "I'm so sorry, Sisters."

I looked at the other Sisters, who were white and shaken. They sat there in shock. I reached for the door and called out, "Open your doors."

I sprang out, glad to be alive.

"God, help us all," prayed Sister Inez Marie, sitting rigid in the middle seat. She turned to me and said, "Pat me on the back, Sister. I can't breathe."

I complied. "That's better," she sighed.

Sister Elisea had already gotten out and thrown up her breakfast. Sister Charlene, alone in the back seat, complained of back pain. I opened the door and reached for her hand. It was cold and clammy. I tried to reassure her, thinking, "She's in shock."

"Don't move unless you feel like it," I warned her. She got out with difficulty.

By then a highway patrol officer had come to inspect the accident. He looked at the slashed tires, the wide skid marks, the broken windshield, the smashed guardrail, and the knocked out posts. Then he pulled a big red bandana out of his hip pocket, and on that cold March day, he mopped perspiration from his brow. He shook his head and said, "You're a lucky crowd of nuns. Your guardian angels were certainly with you that no one was killed here today."

A car of Notre Dame Sisters stopped behind us. Their driver had seen our flat tire and thought it was the extent of our problem, so he offered to take us on to the play. Sister Bernadette directed Sister Marina and me to go with him. Sister Marina was a hot Italian; she didn't want to go to the play at that point. But she went obediently, her eyes blazing.

On the way to Mount Angel, I started to tell the Notre Dame Sisters what had really happened. Sister Marina jabbed me in the ribs and said in a low tone, "Shut up!" Startled, I stopped speaking.

When we passed the Gervais cemetery, one Notre Dame Sister said, "That's where you almost ended up." I felt sick and didn't even smile. How could she be so unfeeling?

At the play, I met my cousin. She is a marvelous listener. I told her all that had happened, and getting it out made me feel better. Sister Marina kept hers all bottled up and went home with a severe headache.

That night we all took sleeping pills, but mine didn't stay down, so I slept badly. All night long, I saw white guardrails and woke myself up by pushing on the bottom of the bed, bracing myself, not wanting to die. This nightmare went on for days, and I began to wonder if I would ever be free of those white guardrails.

Two weeks after the accident, Sister Phyllis came to the basement where I was doing my laundry and asked, "Are you going to Dr. Poole's cabin on Easter Monday with the house?"

"I don't know. I don't feel like it."

"I'll go if you go," she offered.

I looked at her and said, "I just absolutely don't feel like getting into a car again."

"Your life is going to be very limited if you never set foot in a car again," she reasoned.

I stood there, fingering the white collar I was ironing, not wanting to go, yet feeling it would be worse for me if I stayed at home.

"Who's driving?" I ventured.

"Sister Kiernan Mary."

"She wasn't along on that last trip, was she?"

"No, she wasn't."

"Well, maybe it will be all right then. I'll go, Sister Phyllis, but I surely don't feel like it."

"Good! We have to hang together and pull ourselves out of this."

Easter Monday came, and six of us got into the car, with Sister Kiernan Mary driving. Sister Elisea was in the back seat. The trip started out smoothly enough, but I found myself shrinking down in the seat at every curve that had white guardrails.

When we finally arrived at the beach, there was a terrible storm. The wind was howling, and the rain came down in torrents. As we rounded a cliff on a high embankment, someone said, "Oh, look at the ocean!" Sister Kiernan Mary turned her head toward the ocean but kept turning the car around the curve.

Sister Elisea screamed, "Kiernan, watch it!"

I died inside. The intensity of that scream brought back the other accident so vividly, I almost crawled down onto the floor.

I turned to Sister Phyllis. She looked tense and drawn but she squeezed my hand, and that gave me quiet support. However, the memory of that last accident was so vivid, I shrank down, unnerved. I felt depleted and drained. I took a deep breath and gazed out the window, wishing that I had never come and feeling that curves and white guardrails would haunt me for the rest of my days. Yet, I knew that, through it all, God's angels were certainly with us, for we arrived safely.

EXPERIENCES

In 1969, I was stationed in a convent in Portland with eleven other nuns. Six of them went rushing out of the house at 6:30 p.m. for a prayer meeting and didn't return until 12:00 a.m. I thought that was a bit much. I told one of my friends, "Yes, I do believe in praying, but for six hours is a little overboard, don't you think?"

I kept a careful eye on that bunch. They seemed a bit radical. They were friendly enough. In fact, they invited me to their meetings. I thanked them politely and declined. "Too far out," I said, watching from a distance.

One Sister (I'll call her Greta) who went to these meetings was much easier to live with. I remember when Greta first came to our convent. She inspected each unoccupied room and took for herself the choicest pillows, blankets, and lamps. I remember watching her and feeling irked that any nun could be so lacking in the spirit of poverty to not accept whatever was provided in her assigned room. Then, when Greta started going to the prayer meetings, she became kinder and less grabby. That impressed me. But the late meetings really turned me off.

One day, the Sisters who went to the prayer meetings said that Sister Marie had the gift of tongues. I listened to their glowing accounts and wondered about these tongues. So, early one morning when I met Sister Marie in her bathrobe in the hall, I asked her, "Will you speak in tongues for me?"

"Well, it's not like a faucet. You don't just turn it on."

"Oh, I see. I'm sorry," I mumbled, feeling quite disappointed.

She picked up on my disappointment and added, "If you let me pray quietly and recollect myself first, I'll do it for you."

So we both stood there and prayed quietly. Then she prayed in tongues. It was very beautiful and lyrical. It touched something deep inside me.

The next evening, when the six again invited me to go with them to the prayer meeting, I agreed to go, but only as a spectator. I wanted to check this out.

We arrived at Paul Walker's house at about 7:00 p.m. All kinds of people were there: little old grandmothers, young teenagers in bare feet and tight jeans, nuns in full habits, nuns like us in civilian clothing, married folk, toddlers, and even a two-week-old baby. It was a cross-section of the human race, and it was very crowded.

I was given a warm welcome and introduced to many people. As the meeting started, all I wanted was a back seat where I could observe. I sat in a chair partway behind the piano. No one paid any attention to me. They were all very absorbed in praying and singing simple little songs with great reverence and faith. They prayed with their whole beings. It was real.

When they shared testimonies, I was very impressed by two sixteen-year-olds who had gotten off drugs by the power of Jesus. I can still see those radiant faces praising God.

From that night on, I got involved and went to a weekly prayer meeting, first at Paul's house, and later at Loyola Retreat House. It became very natural to pray and sing in tongues and to share on a faith level. I was happy. I met people of all faiths and loved them. I even got healed of white guardrails, and the Holy Spirit helped me to get my driver's license. It is truly amazing what prayer can do—and did do.

Later, we held a charismatic retreat at our Provincial House. Father Brad was one of the leaders. We often prayed in small groups until 12:00 a.m.—and thought nothing of it!

One night, in a tiny chapel by the old novitiate (which we were using for a conference room), Sister Judy and several others prayed individually for me. After that session, I was so excited and happy that I ran all the way up four flights of stairs to write down what had happened. When I got to the dorm, I was careful not to turn on the light and wake those sleeping. At 12:00 a.m., in the pitch black, I grabbed a notebook and, opening it to the middle, wrote what was spoken to me in prophecy:

> *Do not be afraid; I am with you. I have looked into your heart, and I like what I see; I am pleased with you. I will be with you always. I am with you now. I am very much pleased with you, My child. Lean on Me; I will support you. I want your love freely given. I have always loved you. I love you now.*

This message, scribbled in the dark, was readable the next morning. Amazing! The prophecy helped me tremendously. It also helped me to stop judging Greta. The Lord helped me see that my judging her was worse than her snatching the best pillows.

Gradually, I became more Christlike. I met beautiful people of other denominations. I grew to know and appreciate God's goodness in all faiths. It was truly an ecumenical process.

This retreat started me in the process of inner healing for hurts that I had stuffed neatly down inside of me from thirty years back, which were wreaking havoc. Father Brad helped me and gave me this prayer to say daily:

> *Dear Jesus, give me a mind of love for myself as You have for me. Help me to know that I am lovable. Help me to see myself the way You see me. Thank You Jesus, for Your mind of love for me.*

When Father Brad told me I was lovable, I cried. I just couldn't believe that. Gradually, he helped me let Jesus come in. Slowly I was healed as I said the prayer every day. God works ever so gently.

This retreat was a good experience; I was growing through the pain of rejection. I was reaching out to more people. I began to see how God works in the lives of many different types of people.

Shortly after I was healed, I was teaching thirty-one sixth-graders. Among them was a very disturbed, hyperactive boy named Leonard. The other fellows picked on Leonard hatefully. He had a horrible reputation. He slugged a third grader and gave him a bloody nose. Kids and teachers complained incessantly about Leonard. There was never any good news.

I became so undone about his condition that I got a friend, Sister Arlene, to pray daily with me for Leonard.

"How can he ever behave, if everyone expects the worst of him?" I asked Arlene.

"He can't," Arlene said. "We have to build up his self-concept."

"How can we build his self-concept when all I ever hear is 'Leonard hid the first-graders' ball. Leonard pulled out the tulips in the Newtons' front yard. Leonard took the wind-shield wipers off six faculty members' cars. Leonard wrote obscene words in the boys' bathroom.'?"

I got to the point where I didn't want to hear any more "Leonard litanies" of faults. "Enough!" I yelled one day at a complaining teacher. "I don't want to hear any more bad stuff about Leonard!"

"What's the matter? Can't you handle Leonard?"

"Look," I said, still angry, "could you change for the better if all you ever heard were your bad points?"

She paused and blinked. Then she said slowly, "No, I guess I couldn't."

"Well, then how do you expect a little sixth grader to get better if all he gets is beaten down?" I continued.

"You have a point," she conceded.

I continued to praise Leonard and to pray for him. I built him up every chance I got. When he got one math problem right in ten, I talked about the one right one and ignored the others. Sister Arlene praised him every chance she had, as well.

Despite our best efforts, things began sliding downhill. So, one day when he and I were alone together in the class-room, I said, "Sit down, Leonard; we're going to pray."

I fully expected him to laugh at me. He didn't. He looked quite peaceful and sat down willingly. I rejoiced. I gave him the prayer Father Brad had given to me. He promised to say it daily. I told him that he was a good person and that we all make mistakes. I told him God loved him all the time, even when he made mistakes.

He looked at me questioningly and said, "But people don't love me when I make mistakes."

"No," I said, "people are limited. They are not God. They don't understand you completely. Only God does." He seemed satisfied.

I promised him I'd help him all I could. He looked happy and promised me he'd say the prayer every day.

From that time on, things got progressively better. By the middle of the year, one of the teachers who had had the most complaints about Leonard said, "Leonard has a new face. He's not the same boy."

"I agree," I said. "God has given him a new face."

And God continued to help Leonard, and me. I thanked Him daily for the new life He was giving us.

CONCLUSION

After fifty-two years of religious life, I wouldn't trade it for all the technology in America. I am happy. This is where I belong, and this is where I intend to stay. Religious life isn't all fun and games, but Jesus never said it would be. All He ever promised was that He would be with us, and I sincerely believe He is.

I can look back and say, for every superior like Sister Angela Felice, there were at least ten like Sister Ann Marie—caring, helpful, truly mature, religious women.

I remember, when I was beginning as a teacher, I marked 100 percent (A+) on several easy fraction pages in a fifth grader's workbook. Then, when that same fifth grader got her report card, I gave her a D because the other pages of homework that were not in the workbook were practically all F's.

The child's irate mother descended on me and wanted blood—my blood. "Look at this," she demanded, showing the two pages. "How can Susan get a D when she has A's here?"

My wonderful principal, Sister Ann Marie, defended me and pacified the angry parent. Sister Ann Marie also took me aside later and showed me a better way to grade, so this sort of thing didn't happen again. Now it looks like a small thing, but then it was a very big lesson in my life. Sister Ann Marie's support was great.

Only one superior that I had was a health maniac, and my higher superiors rescued me from her. The rest of my superiors were all very sane about health and doctors. The one I mentioned earlier who made a mistake about my back pains was a darling when I ended up needing surgery. She couldn't have been more supportive if she had been the Rock of Gibraltar.

We all grow through our mistakes. Two of the Sisters I lived with while I was under the hypochondriac regime are still my best friends today. We went through fire together, and it fused us into enduring friends.

One principal I had in Portland, in a school of four hundred and fifty pupils, was unusually good. She had a beautiful respect for teachers and children. She worked well with both. I remember how Mark Lehook scribbled up his brand new desk in my sixth-grade room. This principal took Mark to her office with his messed-up desk, gave him the dickens, and made him clean it up. He never forgot. She was very fair, and we had no more messed-up desks.

When I worked as a practical nurse, the Sister RNs were compassionate, caring people who knew how to run the floor. They were always willing to help us rookies, whether it was a backrub or a bed bath that was confusing us.

I owe a big debt of gratitude to my SNJM community

for allowing me to help take care of my sick mother for seven years. She died in August of 1986 at ninety-four-years of age.

I could tell you stories that would make you laugh, like the time a little girl in CCD class, who had learned about face-to-face confession, came running up and said, "Sister, I just went to confession open-faced!"

I could also tell you stories that would make you cry, like the time a sixth-grade boy said to me, "Sister, if they don't like you in this community, you don't have a chance. They just flush you down the drain."

The lovely part is that, through all these ups and downs, God has never abandoned us. It's just like my father, who was ninety-three-years old at the time and tending sixty sheep when he said, "We have to trust in the Lord." I do trust Him and believe He will see me through.

I love being a Sister of The Holy Names of Jesus and Mary. I would not trade places with the Queen of England. I believe that God is very much with us and will continue to bless our charisma of helping people, whether we are teaching children in Oregon or running a clinic in Tutweiler, Mississippi or helping people get housing in Portland, Oregon or caring for the homeless on Burnside or helping prisoners begin their lives anew or praying for an end to terrorism or writing poetry or creating music to feed souls. God is with us.

I believe, if we keep our eyes upon Jesus, He will show us the way.

EARLY DAYS
1935 or so

Mary with cookie

Brothers Bill, George
Vince, Mary playing with deutia flower

EARLY DAYS

George, Ed (neighbor), Vince
Mary

Papa, LeMans, France, WW 1, 1919

FAMILY

Tall corn, 1984
Sister Mary, Papa

Papa's 100th birthday, Feb. 6, 1994
Sister Mary, Papa

TWO VERY GENEROUS NIECES

These two made it possible for me to help take care of
Mom. If I live to be 100, I won't forget them.

Sister Mary, Cindy Steinkamp

Patty Steinkamp
Loving, caring, strong in what counts

VOWS

First vows, 1952
Mom, Sister Mary

Final vows, 1957
Leo, Vince, George, Bill
Mom, Zita, Sister Mary, Papa

THE LONG AND THE SHORT OF IT

Sister Mary on Marylhurst Campus
1952

S. Dona, S. Mary, S. Willetta
1969

FRIENDS, 2002 JUBILEE

S. Mary Lou DiJulio, S. Barbara Bray, S. Mary, S. Donna Van Laeken

Sister Lorna Mae McCormick

S. Mary Lou, S. Barbara, S. Mary

S. Junko Iwasaki from Japan, S. Mary
We lived together for two weeks at
Marylhurst College, became friends,
and still correspond thirty years later

PRAYER FRIENDS

There is something so special about prayer friends.
They are always there for you.

S. Cathy Beckley & S. Mary,
Spokane, July, 2002
S. Cathy has been my friend and
prayer buddy for years

With Shawn Anderson
a prayer friend who is a
wonderful help

Celebrating S. Grace's Birthday
S. Jeanne Concannon, S. Ann Myra, S. Mary
S. Helen Moore, S. Grace Coover, S. Jane Ellen Burns

PRAYER FRIENDS

Jerry and Peggy Barnett, Golden Jubilee, June 2002
I met Jerry at a prayer meeting when I first moved to Portland. I later got to know his wife Peggy, a rare individual. She is madly in love with God and prays her way through everything. She has a vibrant living faith and a terrific sense of humor.

William Christopher "Sax" Mitchell, ASBS, lives in Gary, Indiana, and works in a postal station seven blocks long. About five years ago, he found my reflection book, *River of Life*, on the Internet and ordered one. Although we have never met, we have corresponded ever since. He is a faithful prayer friend and prayed for me every day when I was laid up with ten broken bones.
Sax is a family man with a lovely wife and two fine children. He and his daughter enjoy playing the saxophone. His son excels in art. Sax is an associate of the order of Mother Katherine Drexel Sisters and has many nun friends.

PRAYER FRIENDS

Cecilia Willman ~ dear to my heart. For thirty years, Cecelia Willman and I prayed together. She had a beautiful faith and a very generous heart. It was very hard to let her go to God on Oct. 28, 2000. But what Jesus said to her in her last hours was very inspiring (see below). Cecilia was so strong in Jesus, so loving, so good to be around. I thank God for this friendship and I pray that I too will have her deep faith and love of God.

"Song of my Heart, rest in Me. Know that I am holding you close to My heart as you walk through this dark door. My peace is touching every cell of your body, every part of your soul. Give Me all and let go, dear one. I am calling you home to a better land, to a place of peace and light and joy forever. Your sojourn is over. Your real life is just beginning. Come and be at peace in My arms to enjoy forever the delights of eternity, where there is no fear, no frustration, no pain, no longing for fulfillment, where you have perfection of life, Our Trinity, where you find your beloved family and all tears will be washed away. Peace, My dearest. I am with you."

Shirley, Elaine, S. Mary, Rosemary, Shawn, Morgan

WRITER FRIENDS

Doris Azzopardi, Formosa, Ontario, Canada

Suzanne Renad of South Carolina, who writes
inspiring articles for *Messenger of Sacred Heart*,
with her grandson, Rafe

SISTER MARY, PAST AND PRESENT

1960

1973

Today